CONCERTO IN
FOR OBOE AND ORCHESTRA

Attributed to HAYDN

Edited by Evelyn Rothwell

Piano Reduction by Eric Gritton

NOTE

For every authentic composition by Joseph Haydn there exists one, if not two, spurious works. In the latter part of the eighteenth century Haydn's name worked like magic, and its presence on any manuscript copy or printed edition was enough to ensure the work's success. The manuscript of this oboe concerto, to be found in the Gymnasialbibliothek in Zittau, in the eastern zone of Germany, consists of orchestral parts only. The attribution of the work to Haydn is very doubtful even in the primary source itself; originally the work was anonymous, and Haydn's name was added later and in another hand. That it came to be known at all is only because of the fact that the Haydn scholar Eusebius von Mandyczewski made a score from these parts (the score is now in the library of the Gesellschaft der Musikfreunde in Vienna); and that the *quondam* first oboist of the Vienna Philharmonic Orchestra, Alexander Wunderer, published the work, from Mandyczewski's score, before World War II.

H. C. Robbins Landon

This work has been recorded on Pye CCL 30127 by Evelyn Rothwell with the Hallé Orchestra conducted by Sir John Barbirolli.

INSTRUMENTATION

2 Oboes   2 Horns

2 Trumpets   Timpani

Strings

Duration 21 minutes

Full scores and orchestral parts are on hire

OXFORD UNIVERSITY PRESS
MUSIC DEPARTMENT GREAT CLARENDON STREET OXFORD OX2 6DP

Concerto in C
for Oboe and Orchestra
I

Piano reduction by Eric Gritton

Attributed to HAYDN
edited by Evelyn Rothwell

© 1964 Oxford University Press

OXFORD UNIVERSITY PRESS, MUSIC DEPARTMENT, GREAT CLARENDON STREET, OXFORD OX2 6DP
Photocopying this copyright material is ILLEGAL.

20

II

24

Rondo

III

36